MW00776564

MEDITATIONS AND INDULGENCES

by
Bernard A. McCaffrey, C.S.C.
and
Dr. Kelly Bowring, S.T.D.

Published by:
William J. Hirten Co., Inc.

ACKNOWLEGEMENTS

Nihil Obstat: **Rev. Bryan Patterson**
                        Censor of Books

Imprimatur: **Nicholas DiMarzio, Ph.D., D.D.**
                        Bishop of Brooklyn

Brooklyn, New York   November 10, 2003

The illustrations of the Joyful, Sorrowful and Glorious
Mysteries of the Rosary are reproductions of the original
mosaics at Lourdes, courtesy of Rev. Robert E. Southard.

The Mysteries of Light (Luminous Mysteries) are photographs
of paintings by Carl Heinrich Bloch (*1834-1890*), courtesy of
Det Nationalhistoriske Museum på Frederisborg, Denmark.

Queen of the Most Holy Rosary, pray for us.

TABLE OF CONTENTS

THE ROSARY

THE ROSARY devotion was given to St. Dominic by the Mother of God in the thirteenth century to overcome the heresy of the Albigenses who were materialists much like the Communists of recent years. The Rosary Crusade of Dominic was successful and the Albigenses were defeated. As a result devotion to the Beads spread throughout the Christian world.

The origin of the word "Rosary" is attributed to the vision of the Blessed Virgin seen standing by a young man who was reciting his "AVES." As he said the "HAIL MARYS" the Blessed Virgin gathered roses which issued from his lips, and weaving a crown, placed it on his head. Besides "Rosary" from the Latin "Rosarium" we have "Chaplet," "Garland," "Crown," and from the French "Chapelet."

Throughout history when Christianity or individual Christians have been subjected to the onslaughts of the devil, the Beads have come to save and protect.

"It was not valor, nor arms, nor armies that gave us victory, but Our Lady of the

Rosary," said the Venetian Senate after the Battle of Lepanto. And they were but repeating the words of the Christian sailors.

October 7th 1571

On the seventh of October, 1571, the Christian fleet under the leadership of Don Juan of Austria, son of Charles V of Spain, received Holy Communion and was given the Apostolic Blessing. For three hours before the battle they recited the Rosary. Then began the most gigantic naval engagement ever seen up to that time.

When victory came to the Christian fleet at Lepanto over numerically stronger forces, the Holy Father 500 miles distant, was talking with several Cardinals. Suddenly he arose, walked to the window, and looking towards the East, said "Enough of business, let us thank God for the great victory He has just given our fleet." Pius V's words were recorded, signed and sealed, but kept from the public. Two weeks later, a courier from Venice brought the news of victory.

Our Lady of Victory

In thanksgiving, Pius V instituted the Feast of Our Lady of Victory and granted a Plenary indulgence as often as the people visited the Rosary chapel or altar in a Church where the Rosary Confraternity was established. Pope Gregory XIII later made the Feast that of the Holy Rosary.

ROSARY Feast Extended to Whole Church

In 1683, King John Sobieski III, invoking Our Lady of the Rosary, defeated the Ottoman Turks as they stormed the gates of Vienna and all Western Europe. In 1716, on the Feast of Our Lady of the Snows, Emperor Charles VI , appealing to Our Lady of the Rosary, conquered the Turks at Peterwarden. After another victory on Corfu in 1717, Pope Clement XI extended the Feast of the Holy Rosary to the Whole Church.

THE ROSARY in Modern Times

Coming closer to our own day, we have the example of Pope Leo XIII, the "Pope of the Rosary," who in eleven different encyclical letters on the Rosary urged the Beads as an antidote to the Rationalism and Liberalism of the nineteenth century. Pius XI exhorted its recital in the struggle against Communism and its evils. Pius XII did likewise.

Pope John XXIII, on September 26, 1959, issued an Encyclical on the Rosary, "Grata Recordatio" in which he said, "[For] the rosary is a very commendable form of prayer and meditation. In saying it we weave a mystical garland of Ave Marias, Pater Nosters and Gloria Patris. And as we recite these vocal prayers, we mediate upon the principle mysteries of our religion; the Incarnation of Jesus Christ and the redemption of the human race are proposed, one event after another, for our consideration."

In October 2002, Pope John Paul II issued an apostolic letter addressed to the Bishops, Clergy and Faithful on the Most Holy Rosary (*Rosarium Virginis Mariae*). What follows are excerpts from that letter.

ROSARY OF THE VIRGIN MARY
POPE JOHN PAUL II
October 16, 2002

The Rosary of the Virgin Mary, which gradually took form in the second millennium under the guidance of the Spirit of God, is a prayer loved by countless Saints and encouraged by the Magisterium. Simple yet profound, it still remains, at the dawn of this third millennium, a prayer of great significance, destined to bring forth a harvest of holiness. It blends easily into the spiritual journey of the Christian life, which, after two thousand years, has lost none of the freshness of its beginnings and feels drawn by the Spirit of God to "set out into the deep" (*duc in altum!*) in order once more to proclaim, and even cry out, before the world that Jesus Christ is Lord and Saviour, "the way, and the truth and the life" (*Jn* 14:6), "the goal of human history and the point on which the desires of history and civilization turn".

The Rosary, though clearly Marian in character, is at heart a Christocentric prayer. In the sobriety of its elements, it has all the *depth of the Gospel message in its entirety*, of which it can be said to be a compendium. It is an echo of the prayer of Mary, her perennial *Magnificat* for the work of the redemptive Incarnation which began in her virginal womb. With the Rosary, the Christian people *sits at the school of Mary* and is led to contemplate the beauty on the face of Christ and to experience the depths of his love. Through the Rosary the faithful receive abundant grace, as though from

9

the very hands of the Mother of the Redeemer.

The Rosary,
A Contemplative Prayer

The Rosary, precisely because it starts with Mary's own experience, is *an exquisitely contemplative prayer*. Without this contemplative dimension, it would lose its meaning, as Pope Paul VI clearly pointed out: "Without contemplation, the Rosary is a body without a soul, and its recitation runs the risk of becoming a mechanical repetition of formulas, in violation of the admonition of Christ: 'In praying do not heap up empty phrases as the Gentiles do; for they think they will be heard for their many words' (*Mt* 6:7). By its nature the recitation of the Rosary calls for a quiet rhythm and a lingering pace, helping the individual to meditate on the mysteries of the Lord's life as seen through the eyes of her who was closest to the Lord. In this way the unfathomable riches of these mysteries are disclosed".

Remembering Christ with Mary

Mary's contemplation is above all *a remembering*. We need to understand this word in the biblical sense of remembrance (*zakar*) as a making present of the works brought about by God in the history of salvation. The Bible is an account of saving events culminating in Christ himself. These events not only belong to "yesterday"; *they are also part of the "today" of salvation*.

Christians, while they are called to prayer in common, must also go to their own rooms to pray to their Father in secret (cf. *Mt* 6:6); indeed, according to the teaching of the Apostle, they must pray without ceasing (cf.*1Thes* 5:17)". The Rosary, in its own particular way, is part of this varied panorama of "ceaseless" prayer. If the Liturgy, as the activity of Christ and the Church, is *a saving action par excellence*, the Rosary too, as a "meditation" with Mary on Christ, is *a salutary contemplation*. By immersing us in the mysteries of the Redeemer's life, it ensures that what he has done and what the liturgy makes present is profoundly assimilated and shapes our existence.

Learning Christ from Mary

Christ is the supreme Teacher, the revealer and the one revealed. It is not just a question of learning what he taught but of "*learning him*". In this regard could we have any better teacher than

Mary? From the divine standpoint, the Spirit is the interior teacher who leads us to the full truth of Christ (cf. *Jn* 14:26; 15:26; 16:13). But among creatures no one knows Christ better than Mary; no one can introduce us to a profound knowledge of his mystery better than his Mother.

Contemplating the scenes of the Rosary in union with Mary is a means of learning from her to "read" Christ, to discover his secrets and to understand his message.

This school of Mary is all the more effective if we consider that she teaches by obtaining for us in abundance the gifts of the Holy Spirit, even as she offers us the incomparable example of her own "pilgrimage of faith".

Being conformed to Christ with Mary

Christian spirituality is distinguished by the disciple's commitment to become conformed ever more fully to his Master (cf. *Rom* 8:29; *Phil* 3:10,12). In the words of the Apostle, we are called "to put on the Lord Jesus Christ" (cf. *Rom* 13:14; *Gal* 3:27).

In the spiritual journey of the Rosary, based on the constant contemplation - in Mary's company - of the face of Christ, this demanding ideal of being conformed to him is pursued through an association which could be described in terms of friendship. We are thereby enabled to enter naturally into Christ's life and as it were to share his deepest feelings. In this regard Blessed Bartolo Longo has written: "Just as two friends, frequently in each other's company, tend to develop similar habits, so too, by holding familiar converse with Jesus and the Blessed Virgin, by meditating on the mysteries of the Rosary and by living the same life in Holy Communion, we can become, to the extent of our lowliness, similar to them and can learn from these supreme models a life of humility, poverty, hiddenness, patience and perfection".

In this process of being conformed to Christ in the Rosary, we entrust ourselves in a special way to the maternal care of the Blessed Virgin. Mary is *the perfect icon of the motherhood of the Church*.

Praying to Christ with Mary

Jesus invited us to turn to God with insistence and the confidence that we will be heard: "Ask, and it will be given to you; seek, and you will find; knock, and it will be opened to you" (*Mt* 7:7).

In support of the prayer which Christ and the

Spirit cause to rise in our hearts, Mary intervenes with her maternal intercession. "The prayer of the Church is sustained by the prayer of Mary". If Jesus, the one Mediator, is the Way of our prayer, then Mary, his purest and most transparent reflection, shows us the Way.

Proclaiming Christ with Mary

The Rosary is also *a path of proclamation and increasing knowledge*, in which the mystery of Christ is presented again and again at different levels of the Christian experience. Its form is that of a prayerful and contemplative presentation, capable of forming Christians according to the heart of Christ. When the recitation of the Rosary combines all the elements needed for an effective meditation, especially in its communal celebration in parishes and shrines, it can present *a significant catechetical opportunity* which pastors should use to advantage. In this way too Our Lady of the Rosary continues her work of proclaiming Christ. The history of the Rosary shows how this prayer was used in particular by the Dominicans at a difficult time for the Church due to the spread of heresy. Today we are facing new challenges. Why should we not once more have recourse to the Rosary, with the same faith as those who have gone before us? The Rosary retains all its power and continues to be a valuable pastoral resource for every good evangelizer.

The Rosary, "a compendium of the Gospel"

The only way to approach the contemplation of Christ's face is by listening in the Spirit to the Father's voice, since "no one knows the Son except the Father" (*Mt* 11:27). In order to receive that revelation, attentive listening is indispensable: "Only the experience of silence and prayer offers the proper setting for the growth and development of a true, faithful and consistent knowledge of that mystery".

The Rosary is one of the traditional paths of Christian prayer directed to the contemplation of Christ's face. Pope Paul VI described it in these words: "As a Gospel prayer, centered on the mystery of the redemptive Incarnation, the Rosary is a prayer with a clearly Christological orientation. Its most characteristic element, in fact, the litany-like succession of *Hail Marys*, becomes in itself an unceasing praise of Christ, who is the ultimate object both of the Angel's announcement and of the greeting of the Mother of John the Baptist:

'Blessed is the fruit of your womb' (*Lk* 1:42).

Silence

Listening and meditation are nourished by silence. After the announcement of the mystery and the proclamation of the word, it is fitting to pause and focus one's attention for a suitable period of time on the mystery concerned, before moving into vocal prayer. A discovery of the importance of silence is one of the secrets of practicing contemplation and meditation. One drawback of a society dominated by technology and the mass media is the fact that silence becomes increasingly difficult to achieve.

The "Our Father"

After listening to the word (a Scripture passage related to the Mystery) and focusing on the mystery, it is natural *for the mind to be lifted up towards the Father*. In each of his mysteries, Jesus always leads us to the Father, for as he rests in the Father's bosom (cf. *Jn* 1:18) he is continually turned towards him. He wants us to share in his intimacy with the Father, so that we can say with him: "Abba, Father" (*Rom* 8:15; *Gal* 4:6).

Acting as a kind of foundation for the Christological and Marian meditation which unfolds in the repetition of the *Hail Mary*, the *Our Father* makes meditation upon the mystery, even when carried out in solitude, an ecclesial experience.

The ten "Hail Marys"

This is the most substantial element in the Rosary and also the one which makes it a Marian prayer *par excellence*. Yet when the *Hail Mary* is properly understood, we come to see clearly that its Marian character is not opposed to its Christological character, but that it actually emphasizes and increases it. The first part of the *Hail Mary*, drawn from the words spoken to Mary by the Angel Gabriel and by Saint Elizabeth, is a contemplation in adoration of the mystery accomplished in the Virgin of Nazareth. The repetition of the *Hail Mary* in the Rosary gives us a share in God's own wonder and pleasure: in jubilant amazement we acknowledge the greatest miracle of history. Mary's prophecy here finds its fulfilment: "Henceforth all generations will call me blessed" (*Lk* 1:48).

The center of gravity in the *Hail Mary*, the

hinge as it were which joins its two parts, is *the name of Jesus*. When we repeat the name of Jesus - the only name given to us by which we may hope for salvation (cf. *Acts* 4:12) - in close association with the name of his Blessed Mother, almost as if it were done at her suggestion, we set out on a path of assimilation meant to help us enter more deeply into the life of Christ.

From Mary's uniquely privileged relationship with Christ, which makes her the Mother of God, *Theotókos*, derives the forcefulness of the appeal we make to her in the second half of the prayer, as we entrust to her maternal intercession our lives and the hour of our death.

The "Gloria"

Trinitarian doxology is the goal of all Christian contemplation. For Christ is the way that leads us to the Father in the Spirit. If we travel this way to the end, we repeatedly encounter the mystery of the three divine Persons, to whom all praise, worship and thanksgiving are due. It is important that *the Gloria, the high-point of contemplation*, be given due prominence in the Rosary.

To the extent that meditation on the mystery is attentive and profound, and to the extent that it is enlivened - from one *Hail Mary* to another - by love for Christ and for Mary, the glorification of the Trinity at the end of each decade, far from being a perfunctory conclusion, takes on its proper contemplative tone, raising the mind as it were to the heights of heaven and enabling us in some way to relive the experience of Tabor, a foretaste of the contemplation yet to come: "It is good for us to be here!" (*Lk* 9:33).

The concluding short prayer

In current practice, the Trinitarian doxology is followed by a brief concluding prayer which varies according to local custom. Without in any way diminishing the value of such invocations, it is worthwhile to note that the contemplation of the mysteries could better express their full spiritual fruitfulness if an effort were made to conclude each mystery with *a prayer for the fruits specific to that particular mystery*. In this way the Rosary would better express its connection with the Christian life.

The Rosary beads

The traditional aid used for the recitation of the Rosary is the set of beads. At the most superficial level, the beads often become a simple counting mechanism to mark the succession of *Hail Marys*. Yet they can also take on a symbolism which can give added depth to contemplation.

Here the first thing to note is the way *the beads converge upon the Crucifix*, which both opens and closes the unfolding sequence of prayer. The life and prayer of believers is centered upon Christ. Everything begins from him, everything leads towards him, everything, through him, in the Holy Spirit, attains to the Father.

As a counting mechanism, marking the progress of the prayer, the beads evoke the unending path of contemplation and of Christian perfection. Blessed Bartolo Longo saw them also as a "chain" which links us to God. A chain, yes, but a sweet chain; for sweet indeed is the bond to God who is also our Father. A "filial" chain which puts us in tune with Mary, the "handmaid of the Lord" (*Lk* 1:38) and, most of all, with Christ himself, who, though he was in the form of God, made himself a "servant" out of love for us (*Phil* 2:7).

The opening and closing

The Rosary begins with the recitation of the Creed, as if to make the profession of faith the basis of the contemplative journey about to be undertaken. The Rosary is then ended with a prayer for the intentions of the Pope, as if to expand the vision of the one praying to embrace all the needs of the Church. It is precisely in order to encourage this ecclesial dimension of the Rosary that the Church has seen fit to grant indulgences to those who recite it with the required dispositions.

If prayed in this way, the Rosary truly becomes a spiritual itinerary in which Mary acts as Mother, Teacher and Guide, sustaining the faithful by her powerful intercession. Is it any wonder, then, that the soul feels the need, after saying this prayer and experiencing so profoundly the motherhood of Mary, to burst forth in praise of the Blessed Virgin, either in that splendid prayer the *Salve Regina* or in the *Litany of Loreto*? This is the crowning moment of an inner journey which has brought the faithful into living contact with the mystery of Christ and his Blessed Mother.

"Blessed Rosary of Mary,
sweet chain linking us to God"

The Church has always attributed particular efficacy to this prayer, entrusting to the Rosary, to its choral recitation and to its constant practice, the most difficult problems. At times when Christianity itself seemed under threat, its deliverance was attributed to the power of this prayer, and Our Lady of the Rosary was acclaimed as the one whose intercession brought salvation.

Peace

The grave challenges confronting the world at the start of this new Millennium lead us to think that only an intervention from on high, capable of guiding the hearts of those living in situations of conflict and those governing the destinies of nations, can give reason to hope for a brighter future.

The Rosary is by its nature a prayer for peace, since it consists in the contemplation of Christ, the Prince of Peace, the one who is "our peace" (*Eph* 2:14). Anyone who assimilates the mystery of Christ - and this is clearly the goal of the Rosary - learns the secret of peace and makes it his life's project. Moreover, by virtue of its meditative character, with the tranquil succession of *Hail Marys*, the Rosary has a peaceful effect on those who pray it, disposing them to receive and experience in their innermost depths, and to spread around them, that true peace which is the special gift of the Risen Lord (cf. *Jn* 14:27; 20.21).

As a prayer for peace, the Rosary is also, and always has been, a prayer of and for the family. At one time this prayer was particularly dear to Christian families, and it certainly brought them closer together. It is important not to lose this precious inheritance. We need to return to the practice of family prayer and prayer for families, continuing to use the Rosary.

The family that prays together stays together. The Holy Rosary, by age-old tradition, has shown itself particularly effective as a prayer which brings the family together. Individual family members, in turning their eyes towards Jesus, also regain the ability to look one another in the eye, to communicate, to show solidarity, to forgive one another and to see their covenant of love renewed in the Spirit of God.

... and children

It is also beautiful and fruitful to entrust to this prayer *the growth and development of children.* Does the Rosary not follow the life of Christ, from his conception to his death, and then to his Resurrection and his glory? Parents are finding it ever more difficult to follow the lives of their children as they grow to maturity. In a society of

23

advanced technology, of mass communications and globalization, everything has become hurried, and the cultural distance between generations is growing ever greater. The most diverse messages and the most unpredictable experiences rapidly make their way into the lives of children and adolescents, and parents can become quite anxious about the dangers their children face. At times parents suffer acute disappointment at the failure of their children to resist the seductions of the drug culture, the lure of an unbridled hedonism, the temptation to violence, and the manifold expressions of meaninglessness and despair.

To pray the Rosary *for children*, and even more, *with children*, training them from their earliest years to experience this daily "pause for prayer" with the family, is admittedly not the solution to every problem, but it is a spiritual aid which should not be underestimated.

The Rosary, a treasure to be rediscovered

Dear brothers and sisters! A prayer so easy and yet so rich truly deserves to be rediscovered by the Christian community. Let us do so!

May this appeal of mine not go unheard!

JOHN PAUL II

OUR Lady of Lourdes during her eighteen apparitions followed along on her Beads as Bernadette prayed the Rosary. She joined with Bernadette in the "Glory be to the Father."

Our Lady of Fatima, calling herself the "Lady of the Rosary," said, "Say the Rosary everyday, to bring peace to the world." She also asked that the Rosary be recited every day "with devotion". Later, in connection with the First Saturdays Devotion, Mary requested "meditation on the Mysteries of the Rosary."

The word mediation frightens many people because they regard it as difficult, but Our Blessed Lady would not have asked for it if she thought such was the case. Her invitation should allay any fears we might have.

"Ad Jesum per Mariam... All with Peter to Jesus through Mary," should be our motto St. Josemaria Escriva. Pope John XXIII, in a broadcast to close the Lourdes Marian Year said, "Like our Predecessor, we ardently wish for the renovation of Christianity with a unanimous impulse of Marian piety. When understood according to the doctrine of the Church, this Marian piety cannot help but bring souls more rapidly and securely to Jesus Christ, our only Savior."

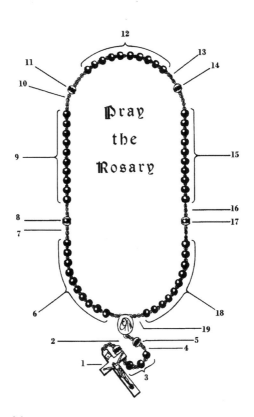

Pray the Rosary

26

HOW TO SAY THE ROSARY

1. Sign yourself
   Kiss the Cross
   Say the Apostles Creed
2. Recite the Our Father
3. Say three Hail Marys
4. Glory be to the Father
   * Fatima Prayer
   Announce first Mystery
5. Recite the Our Father
6. Say 10 Hail Marys
7. Glory be to the Father
   * Fatima Prayer
   Announce second Mystery
8. Recite the Our Father
9. Say 10 Hail Marys
10. Glory be to the Father
    * Fatima Prayer

Announce third Mystery
11. Recite the Our Father
12. Say 10 Hail Marys
13. Glory be to the Father
    * Fatima Prayer
    Announce fourth Mystery
14. Recite the Our Father
15. Say 10 Hail Marys
16. Glory be to the Father
    Fatima Prayer
    Announce fifth Mystery
17. Recite the Our Father
18. Say 10 Hail Marys
19. Glory be to the Father
    * Fatima Prayer
20. Hail Holy Queen Prayer

* O my Jesus, forgive us our sins, save us from the fires of Hell; lead all souls to Heaven especially those who are most in need of Your mercy.

Hail, Holy Queen, Mother of mercy, hail, our life, our sweetness, and our hope! To you do we cry, poor banished children of Eve! To you do we send up our sighs, mourning and weeping in this vale of tears! Turn, then, most gracious advocate, your eyes of mercy towards us; and after this, our exile, show unto us the blessed fruit of your womb, Jesus! O clement, O loving, O sweet Virgin Mary!

O God, by the life, death and resurrection of Your only-begotten Son, You purchased for us the rewards of eternal life; grant, we beseech You, that while meditating on these mysteries of the Holy Rosary, we may imitate what they contain and obtain what they promise. Through the same Christ our Lord. Amen.

PRAYERS OF THE ROSARY

THE APOSTLES' CREED

I BELIEVE in God, the Father Almighty, Creator of heaven and earth; and in Jesus Christ His only Son our Lord; who was conceived of the Holy Spirit, born of the Virgin Mary, suffered under Pontius Pilate, was crucified, died and was buried. He descended into hell; the third day He arose again from the dead; He ascended into Heaven, and sits at the right hand of God the Father Almighty from thence He shall come to judge the living and the dead. I believe in the Holy Spirit, the Holy Catholic Church, the Communion of Saints, the forgiveness of sins, the resurrection of the body and life everlasting. Amen.

OUR FATHER

O UR FATHER, Who art in heaven, hallowed be Thy name. Thy kingdom come; Thy will be done on earth, as it is in heaven. Give us this day our daily bread; and forgive us our trespasses, as we forgive those who trespass against. us. And lead us not into temptation; but deliver us from evil. Amen.

HAIL MARY

HAIL, MARY, full of grace, the Lord is with thee, blessed art thou amongst women and blessed is the fruit of thy womb, Jesus. Holy Mary, Mother of God, pray for us sinners, now and at the hour of our death. Amen.

GLORY BE TO THE FATHER

GLORY be to the Father, and to the Son, and to the Holy spirit. As it was in the beginning is now, and ever shall be, world without end. Amen.

THE FATIMA PRAYER

AFTER each decade may be said the Fatima prayer; "O my Jesus, forgive us our sins, save us from the fires of Hell; lead all souls to Heaven especially those who are most in need of Your mercy."

*The Family That Prays Together
Stays Together.*

A FAMILY CONSECRATION

O Most Sacred Heart of Jesus and Immaculate Heart of Mary! We consecrate to You our family; the _____ family. We proclaim You Jesus our King and Lord. Rule our hearts and souls with Your divine love, which we cherish above all others. Be pleased to guide this family of ours. Take charge! Bless our spiritual and temporal affairs. Sanctify us! Celebrate our joys and comfort us in our sorrows. Keep all evils away from us. Please help us to keep this consecration all the days of our lives. Glory to God our Father; Glory to the Heart of Jesus His son; Glory to the Holy Spirit of divine Love. Amen.

THE JOYFUL MYSTERIES

The Joyful Mysteries commemorate the Infancy, Childhood and Youth of Jesus. They are prayed on Mondays and Saturdays; and sometimes on Sundays in Advent.

THE FIRST JOYFUL MYSTERY
The Annunciation - Gabriel appears to Mary (*Lk* 1:26-38)

"Hail, full of Grace, the Lord is with you.
Blessed art thou among women."

I. THE ANNUNCIATION

O MARY, Queen of Angels, you and Gabriel took part in a conversation which would renew the face of the earth. After your meeting a world formerly steeped in darkness and despair would emerge as one flooded with light and hope. The Angel was God's messenger; you were the representative of humanity. Gabriel asked your consent on behalf of God to be His Mother. After learning that such would be accomplished by the overshadowing of the Holy Spirit with the conception of Jesus in your Immaculate womb, you replied: "May it be done unto me according to thy word.: Becoming a Mother you would remain a Virgin. The Angel's greeting: "AVE MARIA" is the self-same we repeat over and over in the recitation of the Rosary as we say the: "Hail Mary."

Our Father, 10 Hail Marys, Glory be to the Father, Fatima prayer.

Our Lady of the Rosary obtain for me from your Son the grace of humility so that I may recite the Rosary with devotion.

THE SECOND JOYFUL MYSTERY

The Visitation - Mary visits Elizabeth (*Lk* 1:30-56)

"Blessed art thou among women and blessed is the Fruit of thy womb."

II. THE VISITATION

O MARY, Cause of our Joy, you brought great happiness to Elizabeth and her husband, Zechariah, by your visit to their Judean home. St. John the Baptist, "leapt for joy" in his mother's womb at the sound of your greeting. Everyone sought your company for the mere mention of your name spurred relatives, friends and acquaintances on a to a greater love of God. How selfless you were! In your own womb you carried the Maker of the World, but that did not make you proud. Loving everyone, you especially respected the aged. At the same time, you did not forget your vocation as God's Mother when you replied to Elizabeth's greeting with the words of the Magnificat: "My soul magnifies the Lord and my spirit rejoices in God my savior."

Our Father, 10 Hail Marys, Glory be to the Father, Fatima prayer.

Our Lady of the Rosary obtain for me from your Son the Grace of fraternal charity so that I may always put myself out for my neighbor, loving him in God.

THE THIRD JOYFUL MYSTERY
The Nativity - The Birth of Jesus (*Lk* 2:1-14)

"Glory to God in the highest and on earth peace to men of good will."

III. THE NATIVITY

O MARY, Mother of our Creator, your Son at Bethlehem did not despise the poor, the rustic, the simple, the forgotten of the world. Nor did He shun the wealthy and wise of the world as represented by the Magi. They were poor in spirit. He who made the whole world was placed in a manger at birth by you and St. Joseph. Jesus permitted that to happen so that men would not be blinded by His power and glory. He came as one of us and was first seen by shepherds while the dumb animals looked on. To men of good will who received Him as a child He granted "Peace". The Babe loved everyone but not everyone loved Him. Recall to mind Herod who sought His death.

Our Father, 10 Hail Marys, Glory be to the Father, Fatima prayer.

Mary, Queen of the Rosary, as I kneel before the Crib close to you and Joseph, obtain for me from your Son the grace that I may be poor in spirit.

THE FOURTH JOYFUL MYSTERY

The Presentation - Jesus is brought to the Temple (Lk *2:29-32*)

"A light of revelation to the Gentiles, and a glory for thy people Israel."

IV. PRESENTATION OF THE CHILD JESUS IN THE TEMPLE

O MARY Immaculate, you needed no Purification and your Son needed no Redemption but you were obedient to the Law. In accordance with the Mosaic Law a mother was unclean for seven days after the birth of a boy and had to remain home for another thirty-three days. Every firstborn son also had to be offered to the Lord and bought back or "redeemed" by a pair of turtle-doves or two young pigeons. You and Joseph offered the turtle doves. Those were symbolic of the immaculate purity and innocence of Mother and Child. He was Infinite Purity; you, the Immaculate Conception. Anna blessed you, while Simeon prophesied that a sword of sorrow would pierce your soul because of Jesus.

Our Father, 10 Hail Marys, Glory be to the Father, Fatima prayer.

Our Lady of the Rosary obtain for me from your Son the grace of chastity in thought, word and deed, so that I may avoid sins of the flesh.

THE FIFTH JOYFUL MYSTERY

The finding of the Child Jesus in the Temple (*Lk* 2:48-52)

*"And all who were listening to Him were
amazed at His understanding and answers."*

V. THE FINDING OF THE CHILD JESUS IN THE TEMPLE

O MARY, Seat of Wisdom, it was difficult for you to understand the action of Jesus in wandering off from you, Joseph, His relatives and acquaintances without a word to anyone. Your boy, but twelve years old, remained in Jerusalem when you and Joseph started back to Nazareth. Both of you thought He was in the caravan with relatives and friends. Instead He made His way to the Temple, struck up an acquaintance with the doctors of the law and took part in their discussions. They were amazed at His knowledge. You felt proud of Him even though you dutifully expressed your surprise when you asked how He could have left you and Joseph seeking Him with heavy hearts. To which Jesus replied, "Did you not know that I must be about my Father's business?"

Our Father, 10 Hail Marys, Glory be to the Father, Fatima prayer.

Our Lady of the Rosary obtain for me from your Son the grace of zeal so that I may be industrious for the things of God.

PRAYER AFTER THE RECITATION
of the Joyful Mysteries

Let us pray

O GOD, whose only-begotten Son, by His life, death and resurrection has purchased for us the rewards of eternal life, grant, we beseech Thee, that meditating on these mysteries of the most holy Rosary of the Blessed Virgin Mary, we may imitate what they contain and obtain what they promise. Through the same Christ our Lord. Amen.

Queen of the most holy Rosary, pray for us.

O Mary, conceived without sin, pray for us who have recourse to thee.

OUR LADY'S PROMISE

"I PROMISE to assist at the hour of death with the graces necessary for Salvation all those who on the First Saturday of five consecutive months, go to Confession and receive Holy Communion, recite the Rosary, keep me company for a quarter of an hour, while meditating on the Mysteries of the Rosary, with the intention of making Reparation."

THE MYSTERIES OF LIGHT

In his Apostolic Letter, *Rosarium Virginis Mariae*, Pope John Paul II added a new set of mysteries to the Rosary, called the Mysteries of Light. These mysteries include *the Mysteries of Christ's public ministry between His Baptism and His Passion*, whereby He proclaims the Gospel of the Kingdom of God. These five significant moments - called "luminous" mysteries - are *a revelation of the Kingdom now present in the very person of Jesus*. These mysteries are prayed on Thursdays.

THE FIRST MYSTERY OF LIGHT
Jesus' Baptism in the Jordan River (*Mt* 3:13-17)

The Baptism of Jesus, Carl H. Bloch, Oil on canvas 1870
Det Nationalhistoriske Museum på Frederisborg, Denmark

"This is My beloved Son, with Whom I am well pleased."

I. JESUS' BAPTISM IN THE JORDAN RIVER

OMother of the Great King, we pray with you now as we together contemplate the public ministry of the life of Christ. John the Baptist, the greatest Prophet of the Most High, was baptizing sinners with a baptism of repentance for the forgiveness of sins. Jesus appeared in the Jordan and insisted John baptizes Him. As this occurs, the Holy Spirit descended upon Him in the form of a dove while the Father proclaimed, "This is my beloved Son" (*Mt* 3:17). The baptism of Jesus is first of all a mystery of light; it is the Mystery of the Trinity. Here, as Christ descends into the waters, the innocent One who became "sin" for our sake (cf. *2Cor* 5:21) accepts and inaugurates His mission as God's suffering Servant. He submitted entirely to His Father's will and consented out of love to the 'baptism' of His bloody death for the remission of sins. Through His baptism, the heavens are now opened for all!

Our Father, 10 Hail Marys, Glory be to the Father, Fatima prayer.

Our Lady of the Rosary, please obtain for me from your Son the grace to live the vows of my Baptism in union with Jesus my Lord.

THE SECOND MYSTERY OF LIGHT

The Wedding Feast at Cana (*Jn* 2:1-12)

Jesus Changes Water to Wine, Carl H. Bloch, Oil on canvas 1869
Det Nationalhistoriske Museum på Frederisborg, Denmark

"Do whatever He tells you."

II. JESUS' SELF-MANIFESTATION AT THE WEDDING AT CANA

OMother of the Great King, we journey with you to contemplate another mystery of light which is the first of the signs, given at Cana (cf. *Jn 2:1-12*), when Christ changed water into wine and opened the hearts of the disciples to faith. We see in this miracle that marriage is proclaimed henceforth as an efficacious sign of Christ's presence. We also see you Mary in the guise of a teacher and intercessor, as you urge the servants to do what Jesus commands. Thanks to your request at this wedding feast, Most Holy Mother, saying, "Do whatever He tells you" (*Jn 2:5*), we now listen to this great maternal counsel addressed to us today. As Jesus calls you "woman" at Cana, so we see you as the New Eve (*Gen 3:15*), the "woman" with her heart pierced at Calvary (*Jn 19:26*) and the "woman" of the Apocalypse (*Rev 12:1*). Mary, you too assist us against the Evil One. This mystery forms the Marian foundation of all the Mysteries of Light.

Our Father, 10 Hail Marys, Glory be to the Father, Fatima prayer.

Our Lady of the Rosary, please intercede for me to overcome the temptations of the world, the flesh, and the devil so that I may experience the joy of the Lord's presence, power, and love.

THE THIRD MYSTERY OF LIGHT

The Sermon on the Mount (*Lk* 6:17-49)

The Sermon on the Mount, Carl H. Bloch, Oil on canvas 1877
Det Nationalhistoriske Museum på Frederiksborg, Denmark

"Blessed are you poor, for yours is the Kingdom of God."

III. JESUS' PROCLAMATION OF
THE KINGDOM OF GOD

OMother of the Great King, we follow you into the third Mystery of Light to witness the preaching by which Jesus proclaimed the coming of the Kingdom of God. With your maternal guidance, we know that we too are called to enter more fully the Kingdom of God through the Church, the earthly seed and beginning of that Kingdom. As Jesus announced the Kingdom, He called all to conversion (cf. *Mk* 1:15) and forgiveness of sins, saying, "I came not to call the righteous, but sinners" (*Mk* 2:17). We know that Jesus continues to exercise this ministry of mercy until the end of the world, particularly through the Sacrament of Reconciliation which He has entrusted to His Church (cf. *Jn* 20:22-23).

Our Father, 10 Hail Marys, Glory be to the Father, Fatima prayer.

Our Lady of the Rosary, please obtain for me from your Son true and perfect contrition for my sins, sincere sacramental confession in humble trust, and the grace to amend my life for love of God.

THE FOURTH MYSTERY OF LIGHT
The Transfiguration (*Mk* 9:2-8)

The Transfiguration, Carl H. Bloch, Oil on canvas 1872
Det Nationalhistoriske Museum på Frederisborg, Denmark

"This is My beloved Son; listen to Him."

IV. JESUS' TRANSFIGURATION

OMother of the Great King, you who have contemplated His Face more than any other creature, teach us to contemplate Him with the eyes of our hearts, seeing Jesus' beauty as you do. The Transfiguration, traditionally believed to have taken place on Mount Tabor, shows the glory of the Godhead shining forth from the face of Christ. On the threshold of the Passover, Peter, James and John witnessed Jesus' Face and clothes become dazzling with light, as He spoke with Moses and Elijah. The divine glory of Our Lord and the Revelation of the Trinity were revealed, as the voice from Heaven said: "This is My Son, My Chosen; listen to Him!" (*Lk* 9:35). Like the disciples, we are called to prepare to experience with Him the agony of the Passion amid the daily events and the sufferings of our human life, so as to come with Him to the joy of the Resurrection and a life transfigured by the Holy Spirit.

Our Father, 10 Hail Marys, Glory be to the Father, Fatima prayer.

Our Lady of the Rosary, please obtain for me from your Son the grace of His light here on earth so as to enjoy His glory in Heaven.

THE FIFTH MYSTERY OF LIGHT
The Last Supper (*Mk* 14:22-25)

The Last Supper, Carl H. Bloch, Oil on canvas 1876
Det Nationalhistoriske Museum på Frederisborg, Denmark

"Take; This is My Body...This is My Blood."

V. JESUS' INSTITUTION OF
THE HOLY EUCHARIST

OMother of the Great King, we now contemplate with you a final mystery of light when your Divine Son instituted the Holy Eucharist on the night before He died. As the Apostles gathered around the Redeemer at the Last Supper, He washed their feet and gave them the new commandment of love. Christ offers His Body and Blood as food under the signs of bread and wine, instituting a sacrificial memorial of His death and Resurrection for the salvation of the whole world. He testifies "to the end" His love for humanity (*Jn* 13:1) and commands His Apostles (and their successors) to celebrate this Sacrament until His return. From the beginning, the celebration of the Lord's Eucharist has been the center of the Church's life. The Eucharist is the entire Christ (*totus Christus*) - His Body, Blood, Soul, and Divinity - in what is called the Real Presence of Jesus. Through the Eucharist, may we be conformed, united and consecrated to Jesus Christ forever in eternal life.

Our Father, 10 Hail Marys, Glory be to the Father, Fatima prayer.

Our Lady of the Rosary, please obtain for me from your Son the grace to receive Him often in sacramental and spiritual Holy Communion, always worthily and in the spirit of thanksgiving.

PRAYER AFTER THE RECITATION
of the Mysteries of Light

Let us pray

O GOD, whose only-begotten Son, by His life, death and resurrection has purchased for us the rewards of eternal life, grant, we beseech Thee, that meditating on these mysteries of the most holy Rosary of the Blessed Virgin Mary, we may imitate what they contain and obtain what they promise. Through the same Christ our Lord. Amen.

Queen of the most holy Rosary pray for us.

O Mary, conceived without sin, pray for us who have recourse to thee.

THE SORROWFUL MYSTERIES

The Sorrowful Mysteries commemorate the Passion and Death of Jesus. They are said on Tuesdays and Fridays; and sometimes on Sundays during Lent.

THE FIRST SORROWFUL MYSTERY

The Agony in the Garden (*Mt* 26:38-39)

*"And His sweat became as drops of blood
running down upon the ground."*

I. THE AGONY IN THE GARDEN

O LADY of Sorrows, your Son in the Garden of Gethsemane took upon Himself the sins of all mankind. Offering Himself to the Father for us He became the "scapegoat." His very own abandoned Him and one of the Apostles betrayed Him. At the beginning of the Passion the Disciples were in the Garden while He went apart to pray. Three of them, nearby, Peter, James and John fell asleep. They could not watch one hour with Him. Alone your Jesus suffered His agony entreating the Father to let the chalice of suffering pass, if possible, but at the same time He prayed that the will of the Father be accomplished. There on His knees in prayer Jesus sweated blood.

Our Father, 10 Hail Marys, Glory be to the Father, Fatima prayer.

Our Lady of the Rosary, obtain for me from your Son the grace of contrition so that I may grieve over my sins which made Christ suffer.

THE SECOND SORROWFUL MYSTERY

The Scourging at the Pillar (*Jn* 19:1)

*"But Jesus he scourged and delivered
to them to be crucified."*

II. THE SCOURGING

O LADY of Sorrows, I sympathize with you on the terrible scourging your Son endured at the hands of the Roman soldiers. At the ends of their whips were leaden balls which not only cut the skin of Christ but dug into the flesh so that the blood flowed freely and the skin was ripped off. They beat Him almost into unconsciousness. Whenever the Master showed signs of giving way before the inhumane treatment they would desist till He had regained His senses. Then they would begin anew. There was another lashing to which Jesus was subject at the same time. That was the "tongue lashing" coming from their dirty, filthy and foul mouths.

Our Father, 10 Hail Marys, Glory be to the Father, Fatima prayer.

Our Lady of the Rosary obtain for me from your Son the grace of patience so that I may endure all suffering with resignation.

THE THIRD SORROWFUL MYSTERY
The Crowning with Thorns (*Mk* 15:16-17)

"And plaiting a crown of thorns,
they put it upon His head."

III. THE CROWNING WITH THORNS

O LADY of Sorrows, because Jesus had called Himself a King, His enemies mocked, ridiculed and taunted Him. They could not let the opportunity pass. Here was a chance for fun and revenge. Plaiting a crown of thorns they pressed it down on His Head while they clothed Him in a purple robe and placed a reed as a scepter in His Hand. Then in derision they genuflected, bowed down and prostrated before Him, laughing in His Face and spitting into that Sacred Countenance. Taking the reed out of Jesus' Hand they kept striking Him on the Head and across the Face. Jesus sat there as the King of Mercy. The time would come when He would also be the King of Justice.

Our Father, 10 Hail Marys, Glory be to the Father, Fatima prayer.

Our Lady of the Rosary, obtain for me from your Son the gift of mortification so that I may voluntarily suffer physical and spiritual pain for Christ the King.

THE FOURTH SORROWFUL MYSTERY
The Carrying of the Cross (*Jn* 19:17)

*"And bearing the cross for Himself,
He went forth to the place called
the Skull, in Hebrew, Golgotha."*

IV. THE CARRYING OF THE CROSS

OLADY of Sorrows, tearfully you watched the Roman soldiers thrust the heavy wooden Cross upon the Back and Shoulders of Jesus. The Man of Sorrows was one mass of wounds from head to foot. But that did not cause any sympathy on the part of His captors. They beat Him along the Way of the Cross. Everything was permissible so long as He arrived at Calvary, the Hill of the Skulls. For fear that He might collapse before arriving there, they forced Simon of Cyrene to help carry the Cross. Along the way Jesus met you, Mary, at the turning of the street; He fell three times; mercifully He had His face wiped by Veronica who received His image on the veil; and He consoled the holy women with the words: "Weep not for me but for yourselves and your children."

Our Father, 10 Hail Marys, Glory be to the Father, Fatima prayer.

Our Lady of the Rosary, obtain for me from your Son a love of the cross so that I may carry it all the days of my life.

THE FIFTH SORROWFUL MYSTERY

The Crucifixion (*Jn* 19:28-30)

*"And bowing his head,
he gave up his spirit."*

V. THE CRUCIFIXION

O LADY of sorrows, as you stood at the foot of the Cross your heart was breaking. You heard Jesus utter His Last Words. The Master prayed that His Father forgive His enemies because they were ignorant; He promised Paradise to the Good Thief on that very day; He entrusted John to you and you to John in the relationship of Mother and Son; He appealed to the Father for help in His agony; He cried out in thirst; He spoke His "consummation;" and commended His Spirit to the Heavenly Father. Now, Mary, the Prophecy of Simeon is fulfilled! The seventh sword has pierced your heart and you yourself would have died had not God sustained you. St. Longinus, the Roman soldier, thrust the spear into the side of Jesus from which blood and water came forth. Symbolically that represented the birth of the Church.

Our Father, 10 Hail Marys, Glory be to the Father, Fatima prayer.

Our Lady of the Rosary, obtain for me from your Son the grace to be "obedient unto death even to the death of the Cross."

PRAYER AFTER THE RECITATION
of the Sorrowful Mysteries

Let us pray

O GOD, whose only-begotten Son, by His life, death and resurrection has purchased for us the rewards of eternal life, grant, we beseech Thee, that meditating on these mysteries of the most holy Rosary of the Blessed Virgin Mary, we may imitate what they contain and obtain what they promise. Through the same Christ our Lord. Amen.

Queen of the most holy Rosary pray for us.

O Mary, conceived without sin, pray for us who have recourse to thee.

THE GLORIOUS MYSTERIES

The Glorious Mysteries commemorate the Life of the Risen and Heavenly Jesus. They are said on Sundays and Wednesdays.

THE FIRST GLORIOUS MYSTERY
The Resurrection (*Mk* 16:6-8)

*"He is not here, for He has risen
even as He said."*

I. THE RESURRECTION

O MARY, Queen of the Universe, what joy you experience on Easter Sunday when your Divine Son came forth from the tomb without breaking the seals. The Angel rolled back the stone. He told the holy women that Christ had arisen even as He predicted. You did not visit the tomb with those women to anoint the Body because you knew there was no need to do so as He had already visited and showed you the glorified Wounds of victory. Later Jesus manifested Himself to the others: first to Mary Magdalene, then to Peter, to the disciples on the way to Emmaus; and to the Apostles. The following Sunday Thomas the Doubter fell at Christ's Feet with the words "My Lord and my God."

Our Father, 10 Hail Marys, Glory be to the Father, Fatima prayer.

Our Lady of the Rosary, obtain for me from your Son the grace of a renewal of spiritual fervor so that I may realize my richest gift is the Catholic Faith.

THE SECOND GLORIOUS MYSTERY

The Ascension into Heaven (*Acts* 1:10-11)

*"And when He had said this, He was
lifted up before their eyes and
a cloud took Him out of sight."*

II. THE ASCENSION

O MARY, Queen of the Universe, the forty days after the Resurrection were glorious ones for the Infant Church. Jesus in speaking to the Apostles on the shore of Lake Tiberias made Peter the head of the Church and His Vicar on earth. On the Mount in Galilee the Master invested the Apostles with His power, commanding them to "go into the whole world and preach the Gospel to every creature. He that believes and is baptized shall be saved, but he that does not believe shall be condemned." Previously they had received the power to forgive and retain sins in the Sacrament of Penance. With His Mission on earth complete the Savior led them to the top of Mount Olivet, raised His hands to heaven, blessed them and ascended to the Father.

Our Father, 10 Hail Marys, Glory be to the Father, Fatima prayer.

Our Lady of the Rosary, obtain for me from your Son the grace of detachment so that understanding the vanity of worldly things I may adhere to you and heavenly realities.

THE THIRD GLORIOUS MYSTERY
The Descent of the Holy Spirit (*Acts* 2:1-4)

*"And they were all filled
with the Holy Spirit."*

III. THE DESCENT OF THE HOLY SPIRIT

O MARY, Queen of the Universe, ten days after the Ascension, fifty days after Easter, while the Apostles were gathered together with you in the Cenacle for prayer, a mighty wind arose. The Holy Spirit, in the form of tongues of fire, settled over the heads of each Apostle. That wind and fire, symbolizing grace and holiness, initiated the visible mission of the Church. Jesus had promised to send the Holy Spirit who would teach, comfort and assist them. The Apostles received the "Gift of Tongues" so that they could swiftly and effectively carry on their apostolate of conversion. As soldiers of Christ they would soon go to the nations of the world. With them in spirit would be you, Blessed Mother.

Our Father, 10 Hail Marys, Glory be to the Father, Fatima prayer.

Our Lady of the Rosary, obtain for me from your Son the gift of silence so that I may hear the Holy Spirit speaking in the temple that is my body.

THE FOURTH GLORIOUS MYSTERY

The Assumption of Mary into Heaven (*Song of Songs* 2:3-6)

*"Arise, make haste, my love, my dove,
my beautiful one, and come."*

IV. THE ASSUMPTION

O MARY, Queen of the Universe, you lived many years on earth after the Ascension of your Son into Heaven. You were ever torn between the desire of rejoining Jesus above and the need of nourishing the Infant Church here below. Remaining on earth you had the happiness of seeing the Church leaven the world. You witnessed the courage of the Apostles, the Disciples and the Brethren of the Lord, who laid down their lives for the Master. After living many years with St. John the Apostle at Ephesus, Our Lord conducted you Body and Soul to a place at His right Hand. Today we salute you as "Queen Assumed into Heaven."

Our Father, 10 Hail Marys, Glory be to the Father, Fatima prayer.

Our Lady of the Rosary, obtain for me from your Son the grace to desire Heaven above everything in the world --power, wealth, honors.

THE FIFTH GLORIOUS MYSTERY

Mary is crowned Queen of Heaven and Earth. (*Lk* 1:51-54)

*"A woman clothed with the sun,
and the moon was under her feet, and
upon her head a crown of twelve stars."*

V. THE CORONATION

O MARY, Queen of the Universe, you were crowned Queen of Heaven and Earth and your arrival at the throne of God after the Assumption. Just as all creatures are subject to your Son and God by the rule of the Sacred Heart, so He has placed all under your rule of the Immaculate Heart. You are Queen because you are "full of grace," the Mother of Christ, the co-redemptrix. Because you triumphed over the devil, sin, concupiscence and death, Christ, the Mediator between God and Man, has made you the Mediatrix of all Graces, permitting you to dispense all Heavenly blessings to us sinful creatures. Your most powerful prayer is the Rosary. May we say it every day of our life.

Our Father, 10 Hail Marys, Glory be to the Father, Fatima prayer.

Our Lady of the Rosary, obtain for me from your Son the grace of perseverance so that after death I may take my place with the Church Triumphant in Heaven.

PRAYER AFTER THE RECITATION
of the Glorious Mysteries

Let us pray

O GOD, whose only-begotten Son, by His life, death and resurrection has purchased for us the rewards of eternal life, grant, we beseech Thee, that meditating on these mysteries of the most holy Rosary of the Blessed Virgin Mary, we may imitate what they contain and obtain what they promise. Through the same Christ our Lord. Amen.

Queen of the most holy Rosary pray for us.

O Mary, conceived without sin, pray for us who have recourse to thee.

THE 15 PROMISES OF THE ROSARY

Given by the Blessed Virgin Mary to St. Dominic
and Blessed Alan de la Roche.

1. Whoever shall faithfully serve me by the recitation of the Rosary, shall receive signal graces.

2. I promise my special protection and the greatest graces to all those who shall recite the Rosary.

3. The Rosary shall be a powerful armor against hell, it will destroy vice, decrease sin, and defeat heresies.

4. It will cause virtue and good works to flourish; it will obtain for souls the abundant mercy of God; it will withdraw the hearts of people from the love of the world and its vanities, and will lift them to the desire of eternal things. Oh, that souls would sanctify themselves by this means.

5. The soul which recommends itself to me by the recitation of the Rosary, shall not perish.

6. Whoever shall recite the Rosary devoutly, applying himself to the consideration of its Sacred Mysteries shall never be conquered by misfortune. God will not chastise him in His justice, he shall not perish by an unprovided death; if he be just, he shall remain in the grace of God, and become worthy of eternal life.

7. Whoever shall have a true devotion for the Rosary shall not die without the Sacraments of the Church.

8. Those who are faithful to recite the Rosary shall have during their life and at their death the light of God and the plenitude of His graces; at the moment of death they shall participate in the merits of the Saints in Paradise.

9. I shall deliver from purgatory those who have been devoted to the Rosary.

10. The faithful children of the Rosary shall merit a high degree of glory in Heaven.

11. You shall obtain all you ask of me by the recitation of the Rosary.

12. All those who propagate the Holy Rosary shall be aided by me in their necessities.

13. I have obtained from my Divine Son that all the advocates of the Rosary shall have for intercessors the entire celestial court during their life and at the hour of death.

14. All who recite the Rosary are my children, and brothers and sisters of my only Son, Jesus Christ.

15. Devotion of my Rosary is a great sign of predestination.

INDULGENCES FOR
PRAYING THE ROSARY

An indulgence is defined in the *Code of Canon Law* (can.992) and in the *Catechism of the Catholic Church* (n. 1471): "An indulgence is a remission before God of the temporal punishment due to sins whose guilt has already been forgiven, which the faithful Christian who is duly disposed gains under certain prescribed conditions through the action of the Church which, as the minister of redemption, dispenses and applies with authority the treasury of the satisfactions of Christ and the saints." In general, the gaining of indulgences requires certain prescribed *conditions* (see E below), and the performance of certain (charitable) *works* (like the praying of the Holy Rosary).

An indulgence is either PLENARY or PARTIAL, depending upon whether it frees one from the whole or from a part of the temporal punishment due to sin.

RECEIVING AN INDULGENCE

A plenary indulgence is granted, if the Rosary (5 decades) is recited in a church or public oratory or in a family group, a religious community or pious association; a partial indulgence is granted in other circumstances.

Also to gain the plenary indulgence, the following must be performed:

A. Five decades of the Rosary must be prayed continuously.

B. The prayers of the Rosary must be prayed vocally and one must meditate on the Mysteries of the Rosary.

C. If the recitation of the Rosary is public, the Mysteries of the Rosary must be announced.

D. A plenary indulgence can be gained only once a day.

E. To gain a Plenary Indulgence, three other conditions must be filled:

1. A sacramental confession (within about 20 days of the indulgence, and one confession suffices for many days of indulgences provided the participant remains in grace).

2. Worthy reception of Eucharistic Communion.

3. Prayers for the Pope's intentions (Our Father, Hail Mary, and Glory Be or Apostles' Creed).

In addition, one must be free of all attachment to sin, even venial sin. If this is not present or if all the above conditions are not fulfilled, the indulgence is only partial.

F. Both the plenary and partial indulgences may be applied to either oneself or to a deceased person in Purgatory, but they cannot be applied to other persons living on earth.

TEACHINGS OF POPE JOHN PAUL II ON INDULGENCES

I strongly urge priests to teach the faithful, with appropriate and intensive catechesis, to take advantage of the great good of indulgences according to the mind and heart of the Church. (4/1/00)

Experience shows, in fact, that indulgences are sometimes received with superficial attitudes that ultimately frustrate God's gift and cast a shadow on the very truths and values taught by the Church...

The starting-point for understanding indulgences is the abundance of God's mercy revealed in the Cross of Christ. The crucified Jesus is the great "indulgence" that the Father has offered humanity through the forgiveness of sins and the possibility of living as children (cf. *Jn* 1:12-13) in the Holy Spirit (cf. *Gal* 4:6; *Rom* 5:5; 8:15-16)… In the light of this principle, it is not difficult to understand how reconciliation with God, although based on a free and abundant offer of mercy, at the same time implies an arduous process which involves the individual's personal effort and the Church's sacramental work. For the forgiveness of sins committed after Baptism, this process is centered on the Sacrament of Penance, but it continues after the sacramental celebration. The person must be gradually "healed" of the negative effects which sin has caused in him (what the theological tradition calls the "punishments" and "remains" of sin).

At first sight, to speak of punishment after sacramental forgiveness might seem inconsistent. The Old Testament, however, shows us how normal it is to undergo reparative punishment after forgiveness.

God's fatherly love does not rule out punishment, even if the latter must always be understood as part of a merciful justice that re-establishes the violated order for the sake of man's own good (cf. *Heb* 12:4-11).

In this context temporal punishment expresses the condition of suffering of those who, although reconciled with God, are still marked by those "remains" of sin which do not leave them totally open to grace. Precisely for the sake of complete healing, the sinner is called to undertake a journey of conversion towards the fullness of love.

In this process God's mercy comes to his aid in special ways. The temporal punishment itself serves as "medicine" to the extent that the person allows it to challenge him to undertake his own profound conversion. This is the meaning of the "satisfaction" required in the Sacrament of Penance.

The Church has a treasury, then, which is "dispensed" as it were through indulgences. This "distribution" should not be understood as a sort of automatic transfer, as if we were speaking of "things." It is instead the expression of the Church's full confidence of being heard by the Father when - in view of Christ's merits and, by His gift, those of Our Lady and the Saints - she asks him to mitigate or cancel the painful aspect of punishment by fostering its medicinal aspect through other channels of grace. In the unfathomable mystery of divine wisdom, this gift of intercession can also benefit the faithful departed, who receive its fruits in a way appropriate to their condition.

We can see, then, how indulgences, far from being a sort of "discount" on the duty of conversion, are instead an aid to its prompt, generous and radical fulfillment. This is required to such an extent that the spiritual condition for receiving a plenary indulgence is the exclusion "of all attachment to sin, even venial sin" (*Enchiridion Indulgentiarum*).

Therefore, it would be a mistake to think that we can receive this gift by simply performing certain outward acts. On the contrary, they are required as the expression and support of our progress in conversion. They particularly show our faith in God's mercy and in the marvelous reality of communion, which Christ has achieved by indissolubly uniting the Church to Himself as His Body and Bride. (9/29/99)

OTHER WAYS TO RECEIVE
AN INDULGENCE

Remember that a plenary indulgence is granted for any one of the following (with all the other conditions completed):

- Adoration of the *Blessed Sacrament* for at least a half-hour

- Pious reading of *Sacred Scripture* for at least a half-hour

- Praying the *Stations of the Cross*

- Praying the *Holy Rosary* in common or in church.

THE "54-day ROSARY NOVENA"

THE "54-day Rosary Novena" is an uninterrupted series of Rosaries in honor of Our Lady, revealed to the incurably sick Fortuna Agrelli by Our Lady of Pompeii at Naples in 1884. On March 3rd of that year, after Fortuna and her relatives had begun a novena of Rosaries for a cure, Our Blessed Mother appeared to her saying; "Make three novenas and you will obtain your request."

Later Our Blessed Lady said to her: "Whoever wishes to receive favors from me should make three novenas of the prayers of the Rosary in petition and three novenas in thanksgiving."

The devotion consists of the Rosary of petition said every day for twenty-seven days; then regardless of whether or not you have received your request immediately begin the Rosary of thanksgiving every day for twenty-seven days.

NOVENA IN HONOR OF OUR LADY OF THE MIRACULOUS MEDAL
Novena Prayer

O Immaculate Virgin Mary, Mother of Our Lord Jesus and our Mother, penetrated with the most lively confidence in your all powerful and never failing intercession, manifested so often through the Miraculous Medal, we your loving and trustful children implore you to obtain for us the graces and favors we ask during this Novena, if they be beneficial to our immortal souls, and the souls for whom we pray.

You know, O Mary, how often our souls have been the sanctuaries of your Son who hates iniquity. Obtain for us then a deep hatred of sin and that purity of heart which will attach us to God alone so that our every thought, word and deed may tend to His greater glory. Obtain for us also a spirit of prayer and self-denial that we may recover by penance what we have lost by sin and at length attain to that blessed abode where you are the Queen of angels and of men. Amen.

NOVENA PRAYERS

The Novena Prayers found below are an ideal way of preparing for great feast days in the Church. Certainly, if one recites a Novena Prayer, short though it be, for nine days before a great feast, he or she will come to that day far better prepared to enter into the mystery being celebrated than one who barely adverts to the feast.

THE ANNUNCIATION
March 25

This novena begins on March 16.

Hail Mary, full of grace, The Lord is with you.

Let us pray. O God, by your divine decree the Word was made flesh in the womb of the blessed Virgin Mary at the announcement of the angel. May her prayers help us, for we believe that she is truly the Mother of God. Through Christ our Lord. Amen.

THE VISITATION
May 31

This novena begins on May 22.

Blessed are you among women, And blessed is the fruit of your womb.

Let us pray. Grant us your servants the gift of your divine grace, O Lord. Let the solemn feast of the blessed Virgin's Visitation establish us more securely in peace, just as her motherhood heralded the beginning of our salvation. Through Christ our Lord. Amen.

OUR MOTHER OF PERPETUAL HELP
June 27

This novena begins on June 18.

Virgin Mother of Christ, assist the needy who resort to you. Give comfort to all who trust in your help.

Let us pray. O Lord Jesus Christ, we venerate the wondrous picture of your Mother, Mary. You gave her to be our mother also, always ready to help us. Grant that we who earnestly implore her motherly assistance may be worthy to enjoy the eternal fruit of your redemption. You live and reign forever and ever. Amen.

THE ASSUMPTION
August 15

This novena begins on August 6.

The holy Mother of God has been taken up to heaven. Above the choirs of angels to the kingdom of her Son.

Let us pray. O almighty and eternal God, you have taken into heavenly glory the body and soul of the immaculate Virgin Mary, the Mother of your Son. May we always look upward toward heaven and come to be worthy of sharing her glory. Through Christ our Lord. Amen.

THE BIRTH OF MARY
September 8

This novena begins on August 30.

This day is the birthday of the blessed Virgin Mary.

Her life brings glory to the Church around the world.

Let us pray. Grant your servants the gift of your divine grace, O Lord. Let the solemn feast of the blessed Virgin's nativity establish us more securely in peace, just as her motherhood heralded the beginning of salvation. Through Christ our Lord. Amen.

THE PRESENTATION OF MARY
November 21

This novena begins on November 12.

Let me praise you, O most holy Virgin Mary. Give me strength when I encounter your foes.

Let us pray. O God, you willed that the blessed ever-virgin Mary, the dwelling place of the Holy Spirit, should be presented in the temple on this day. May we be worthy through her intercession to be presented in the temple of your glory. Through Christ our Lord. Amen.

THE IMMACULATE CONCEPTION
December 8

This novena begins on November 29.

This day marks the Immaculate conception of the blessed Virgin Mary. With her virginal foot she crushed the serpent's head.

Let us pray. O God, by foreseen merits of the death of Christ, you shielded Mary from all stain of sin and preserved the Virgin Mother immaculate at her conception so that she might be a fitting dwelling place for your Son. Cleanse us from sin through her intercession so that we may also come to you untainted by sin. Through Christ our Lord. Amen.

PRAYER TO OUR LADY OF GUADALUPE

Our Lady of Guadalupe, mystical rose, make intercession for the Holy Church, protect the Sovereign Pontiff, help all those who invoke you in their necessities, and since you are the ever Virgin Mary and Mother of the true God, obtain for us from thy most holy Son the grace of keeping our faith, sweet hope in the midst of the bitterness of life, burning charity and the precious gift of final perseverance. Amen.

THE MEMORARE OF ST. BERNARD

Remember, O most gracious Virgin Mary, that never was it known that any one who fled to your protection, implored your help, and sought your intercession, was left unaided. Inspired with this confidence, I fly unto you, O Virgin of virgins, my Mother, to you I come, before you I stand sinful and sorrowful. O Mother of the Word Incarnate! despise not my petitions, but, in your mercy, hear and answer me. Amen.

THE MAGNIFICAT

My soul proclaims the greatness of the Lord,
my spirit rejoices in God my Savior
for he has looked with favor on his lowly servant.

From this day all generations will call me blessed:
the Almighty has done great things for me,
and holy is his Name.

He has mercy on those who fear him
in every generation.

He has shown the strength of his arm,
he has scattered the proud in their conceit.

He has cast down the mighty from their thrones,
and has lifted up the lowly.

He has filled the hungry with good things,
and the rich he has sent away empty.

He has come to the help of his servant Israel
for he has remembered his promise of mercy,
the promise he made to our fathers,
to Abraham and his children forever.
(*Lk 1:46-55*)

SAINTS ON THE ROSARY

"After the Holy Sacrifice of the Mass, there is nothing in the Church that I love as much as the Rosary." *Our Lady to Blessed Alan de la Roche.*

"If you want peace in your heart, in your home, in your country, assemble together every night and say the Rosary." *Pope St. Pius X.*

"The Rosary is a priceless treasure inspired by God." *St. Louis Mary de Montfort.*

"Now that we are forced to speak we must also tell you this: Nobody who perseveres in saying the Rosary will be damned, because she obtains for her servants the grace of true contrition for their sins and by means of this they obtain God's forgiveness and mercy." *The devils to St. Dominic.*

The Jesuits in Hiroshima and the Franciscans in Nagasaki, during the dropping of the atomic bombs on Japan in WWII, were miraculously spared because, according to one, "In [our] house the Rosary was prayed every day. In that house, we were living the message of Fatima."

"I would be willing to return to a life of suffering until the end of time to merit the degree of glory which God rewards one devoutly recited Hail Mary prayer."
St. Teresa of Avila after death in a vision to one of her religious sisters.

St. Pio of Pietrelcina the stigmatic priest said: "The Rosary is **THE WEAPON**."

The Rosary and the Brown Scapular are inseparable. Our Lady revealed to St. Dominic: "One day through the Rosary and the Scapular I will save the world."

Printed in Hong Kong